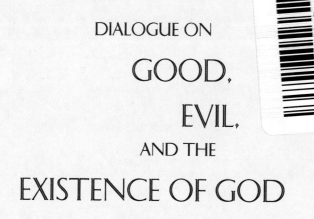

DIALOGUE ON

GOOD,

EVIL,

AND THE

EXISTENCE OF GOD

DIALOGUE ON

GOOD,

EVIL,

AND THE

EXISTENCE OF GOD

John Perry

Hackett Publishing Company, Inc.
Indianapolis/Cambridge

05 04 03 02 01 00 99   1 2 3 4 5 6

Cover design by Abigail Coyle and Deborah Wilkes
Interior design by Meera Dash

For further information, please address

Hackett Publishing Company, Inc.
P.O. Box 44937
Indianapolis, IN 46244-0937

www.hackettpublishing.com

Library of Congress Cataloging-in-Publication Data

Perry, John, 1943–
    Dialogue on good, evil, and the existence of God / by John Perry.
        p. cm.
    Includes bibliographical references.
    ISBN 0-87220-460-X (pbk.).—ISBN 0-87220-461-8 (cloth)
    1. Good and evil.   2. Theodicy.   I. Title.
    BJ1401.P46   1999
    214—dc21   99-30951
                                                    CIP

to the faculty and students of Doane College,
where I came to love philosophy

CONTENTS

INTRODUCTION

Gretchen Weirob, Sam Miller, and Dave Cohen are my inventions. I think of them as having a life beyond these *Dialogues*, however, that explains how they came to be written. When Weirob, Miller, and Cohen had philosophical conversations, Miller kept fairly detailed notes. He wrote these notes up in a rather dry fashion, which focused on the arguments. Dave Cohen gave me a lot of information about how the conversations actually went, and of course, I have my own memories of Gretchen. These are the sources I have used to reconstruct this dialogue and its counterpart, *A Dialogue on Personal Identity and Immortality*.

Given Sam's methodical ways, it is surprising that his notes on these conversations were so scattered about. But as it turned out, the notes were inserted in the copies of books they had discussed in the conversations. The notes for the other *Dialogue* were found in Sam's copy of Locke's *Essay*, which I borrowed from his library not long after he died. I had no idea that Sam had saved notes of other conversations until a couple of years ago, when the task of sorting all of his books fell to me. The notes for this conversation were found in his copy of Augustine's *Confessions*.

DIALOGUE ON GOOD, EVIL, AND THE EXISTENCE OF GOD

Characters: Gretchen Weirob, Sam Miller, Dave Cohen

1

THE FIRST MORNING

MILLER: Hello, Gretchen. I stopped by because I heard that you were under the weather. I brought you a cup of coffee and a cinnamon roll from Starbucks.

WEIROB: That was most kind of you, Sam. I've got a terrible case of the flu, and I feel absolutely miserable. I'm sneezing and dripping; every muscle aches; I've got a headache. I know that coffee will help my headache, but I haven't had the willpower to get up and make myself some. Your kindness is most welcome.

MILLER: To be honest, I also thought you might like someone to talk to for a while. But if you have a headache . . .

WEIROB: Oh, no, not at all. Coffee and good conversation will make me forget my misery—better than aspirin, and not as hard on the stomach.

MILLER: I suspected as much. In fact, I suggested to Dave Cohen that he drop by after his class—by then we'd be sure to be in the middle of something interesting.

Gretchen, would it be stretching my kindness beyond what you could endure if I were to offer to say a prayer for your speedy recovery?

WEIROB: I think I'll pass on that, Sam.

MILLER: I know you're not exactly a confirmed believer in God.

WEIROB: It's not just that. Suppose I were. Suppose I believed in your Christian God. Just how do you think a prayer would help? Do you think God doesn't *know* that I have the flu and am miserable? God *must* know that I am miserable, for according to you he knows everything. In fact, not only does he know that I am miserable, but he also knows that you would like to see me get better. So how in the world does a prayer help? You simply would be communicating to God what God already knows, thereby wasting God's time and yours. Not to mention mine.

MILLER: I can see I'm in for a full-scale assault on everything I believe and hold dear. A small price to pay, I guess, if it helps your headache. You're clearly feeling better by the moment, so you may as well continue.

WEIROB: You think that if you pray, God may make me better. Well, God certainly can make me feel better, since he is (supposedly) all-powerful. But then why hasn't he done this already?

MILLER: The true value of prayer would be its effect on us, not any effect on God. It would remind us that however bad you feel, however much you sneeze, however achy your limbs, however much your head hurts, we are in the hands of a loving, beneficent God.

WEIROB: Then please spare me your prayer. You admit that it won't help get rid of my flu. And even if I believed that we were in the hands of a loving, beneficent God, which I thoroughly doubt, I certainly wouldn't want to be reminded of it.

MILLER: Why not?

WEIROB: Because that would mean that a loving, all-powerful, all-knowing God finds it reasonable to let me suffer. Now why would that be so? Any reason I can think of is extremely depressing. Is it that I am so completely small and insignificant that even an omnipotent and omniscient Being doesn't notice? Or that I am so disgusting that it is actually a good thing that I am suffering? Or that I am so confused about what is good and bad that what seems to be a completely gratuitous evil—indeed, a whole series of them, from achy, drizzly head to achy, tired legs—is really a good thing, perhaps something your God is proud of? Maybe he feels about my flu like we feel about a nice sunrise—a beautiful beginning to a perfect day. "Oh, wow," he may be saying, "what a nice way to start the day. We'll have a beautiful sunrise and I'll make that little twit Gretchen Weirob sore and drippy and headachy." I declare, Sam, sometimes it is more than I can bear thinking that you really believe in such a monster.

MILLER: So, is your mind off your headache yet?

WEIROB: Yes, I admit that it is, but no thanks to any prayer of yours. No one can worry about their head for long when philosophy beckons, and what better for a tired, achy philosopher than arguing against a God such as yours. It's like shooting fish in a barrel.

MILLER: Go ahead and shoot your fish. I'll just do my best. Anything to get your mind off your misery.

WEIROB: OK, try hard to overcome your emotional commitment to your religion, and just look at it as a straightforward, logical, philosophical proposition. You believe in a God that is perfect in every way. All-knowing, all-powerful, and benevolent. That's what it says in some of the creeds I had to learn as a child, words that are etched in my brain. But how can this be? If your God exists, he knows I have the flu because he knows everything. He can certainly make it the case that I cease to have the flu, or could have prevented me from having the flu in the first place, for he is all-powerful. But I *do* have the flu! What am I to conclude? He must not care. But shouldn't a really benevolent God care about even a wretch like me? Why would he *want* me to suffer? But if he doesn't want me to suffer, why am I suffering? Like I said, shooting fish in a barrel. If I accept your Christian premise, that this world and all that is in it is the creation of a perfect God, all-knowing, all-powerful, and completely benevolent, I must draw the conclusion that I am not suffering. But I am suffering. So I reject the premise. There is no being that meets your definition of God. Perhaps there is no God. Or perhaps there is, but he is ignorant, or weak, or mean.

MILLER: Gretchen, you must know that this argument— the so-called problem of evil—is at least as ancient as Augustine. Augustine tells us in his *Confessions* that it was only when he figured out how a world created by a Christian God could contain evil that he converted to Christianity.

WEIROB: Converted from what?

MILLER: He had been a Manichaean—Manichaeans believe that there are two ultimate principles controlling the world, good and evil. Our world is their battleground. According to the Manichaeans, the evil parts of the world are not due to God, that is, the good force. They are due to the other force, evil, or the dark force.

WEIROB: That sounds pretty reasonable. Would you be satisfied if I became religious, but became a Manichaean rather than a Christian? From the way you describe Manichaeism, maybe I could take the *Star Wars* movies as my sacred text.

MILLER: No, Gretchen, I would not.

WEIROB: I've long admired Augustine—he's the author of my favorite prayer.

MILLER: Your favorite prayer? I'm surprised that you know anything about Augustine. But I'm absolutely flabbergasted that you have a favorite prayer. How does it go?

WEIROB: "Lord, give me chastity . . . but not yet!"

MILLER: Oh, Gretchen!

WEIROB: You must admit that it is a prayer, and it is from Augustine.

MILLER: Yes, I guess so. It's a request directed at God, and Augustine definitely said it—he planned to become a member of a community where celibacy was expected of serious Christians. His plea had a serious point, which you presumably missed—that even when he was intellectually convinced that Christianity was the true religion, he still needed God's grace to complete the conversion.

WEIROB: That's all very interesting, Sam, but frankly, when you mention the word *grace* I feel my headache coming back. I take it that you think Augustine's intellectual conversion resulted from a real insight about the problem of evil. Tell me about that.

MILLER: Yes, I think he showed that your argument—that an all-perfect God can't exist because there is evil—is as full of holes as a piece of Swiss cheese.

WEIROB: That will take some convincing. I know that the problem must be old, for Augustine lived a millennium and a half ago. Age doesn't make the argument bad, nor does the fact that a saint thought it was. In fact, the problem of evil is like a bottle of fine wine. It gets *better* with age. It has made Christians like Augustine and you squirm for centuries. So much the better for it. So where are these holes?

MILLER: You don't expect me to convince you of the existence of a Christian God, do you? I wouldn't take that on.

WEIROB: No, just convince me that that Christian God you believe in—all-perfect, omnipotent, omniscient, and benevolent—could possibly exist, even given as unimportant a bit of suffering as my flu. Do that, and I'll let you say a prayer for me.

MILLER: That's a challenge worth taking on.
          The main point to be made really is just a logical one, that a thing can be better for having a part or an aspect that, considered out of context, is of little value, or even ugly. For example, a novel as a whole can be more interesting because it has a dull chapter—if that dull chap-

ter is necessary for setting up the situations that make the rest of the novel intricate and interesting. A painting can be more beautiful for having a patch of color that is, in itself, quite ugly and unattractive. And so forth. So a world can contain a little evil in it, or even a lot, but this may, in the grand scheme of things, just be a necessary part of the world, something that contributes to the goodness of it, that makes it better than it would be otherwise. That seems clear enough to me. But somehow I doubt that you are ready for my prayer.

WEIROB: Not quite yet, if you don't mind. Frankly, I don't feel like an ugly patch of color in a great painting, or a dull chapter in a good novel, or a discordant note in a great symphony—that's one you didn't mention, by the way. I don't think my suffering with this damn flu compares with those examples at all. I'm not here to be heard or witnessed by someone else, am I? I'm not part of a play or a novel or a painting.

I can see that someone might paint a picture of me that would be, if not exactly ugly, not much to look at on its own. And I can see that such a picture might enhance the overall aesthetic value of a larger picture of which it was a part. Perhaps there is a picture of a number of quite different-looking people and the overall effect is quite stunning, reminding us of the diversity of human nature—or something like that—in a way that none of the pictures by themselves could have done. It might be that the big painting would be a reasonable thing to hang on a wall, even though none of its parts— the individual portraits—would be worth hanging as separate paintings. Perhaps a quite beautiful or moving picture might include a part that depicted me sneezing and sniffling. Who knows? But that seems quite irrelevant to the question at hand. I'm not a picture of a sniveling, dripping, suffering human; I *am* a sniveling, dripping, suffering human.

MILLER: Perhaps there are better examples. Think of the times we go fishing. Surely it is some form of mild suffering to get out of bed before dawn on a chilly Nebraska spring morning when one might sleep in. But the days as a whole, the days that start out with those unpleasant experiences, are some of the most enjoyable days one can imagine. The point has nothing to do really with pictures or novels or symphonies. Given any kind of whole—a whole picture, a whole ball game, a whole day, a whole life, a whole world—parts that wouldn't be very good were they to exist in isolation contribute to the whole in such a way that the whole is better with these parts than without them.

WEIROB: Ball game? That's a new one.

MILLER: For example, an error in an early inning—a bit of imperfect playing—may be just the lucky break that inspires a weak team and produces a thrilling game—to the participants, not only the spectators.

WEIROB: I get the idea. I'm really not sure what to say. I wonder what a baseball game would be like if all the players were perfect—if perfect pitchers and fielders were up against perfect batters and runners—well, it's really hard to say, isn't it? It seems as if perfect pitchers could strike out anyone, and perfect batters could hit anything.

MILLER: I think we'd better go back to the fishing example.

WEIROB: OK. The point there was that what one can call a fine day, perhaps even a "perfect" day in a loose sense, can contain a part that isn't that much fun, that might even qualify as a bit of suffering. And the blend of misery and pleasure doesn't have to do with the effect on some outsider who watches and appreciates this combination at work—as in the cases of the novel and the picture. It is the participants whose own lives are better in virtue of their own misery who matter—that's your point.

MILLER: Yes. And of course there are lots of examples of hard work and sacrifice at any stage in a person's life being the condition of great success, comfort, and satisfaction at another stage. Think of the sacrifices that medical students make, and the satisfactions that come later, after they become practicing physicians.

WEIROB: You mean charging outrageous fees and playing golf on Wednesday afternoons?

MILLER: You can jest, Gretchen, but the point is a logical one. Take any whole, a whole day, a whole year, a whole life. Just because some creatures some of the time feel some discomfort, or even suffer, does not mean that the whole day, or the whole life, may not be a fine one, and that the discomfort or suffering may not have been necessary for the quality of the day or the life as a whole. But what goes for a day or a life, goes for the world as a whole. Just as we have a plan for spending a fine day fishing that has, as a necessary part, a little suffering early in the morning, so God may have a plan for the world that requires suffering. It still may be a fine world, a much better world than it would have been without the suffering.

WEIROB: Please excuse me for not being convinced.

Let's start with the fishing example. Of course I can see that we can have a fine day, what we would call a perfect day, that contains some pain and discomfort. It's a pain to get up as early as one has to, if one is going to catch the fish in a cooperative mood. No day of fishing goes by—for me, at least—without at least once hooking my own finger while trying to bait the hook. Still, such days are perfect days.

But what do we mean by that? We mean that they are among the nicest days we expect to have. Days that are as perfect as we imagine that days can ever be. But not really perfect. When I say as perfect as a day can be, I mean as perfect as a day can be, given the way the world works. Given that it's hard to get up in the morning, given that fish are more likely to bite in the morning than in the afternoon, given that I'm clumsy and fishhooks are sharp—given all of that, sure, such a day is as fine a day as one can imagine, or ranks right up there at any rate.

But where did all of those givens come from? Who is responsible for the fact that it's hard to get up in the morning? We can imagine a world in which everyone hops out of bed fresh as a daisy and happy that it is morning. Some people I know claim that they are like that. I don't believe them, but it's at least possible that there should be such people, and even that I should be one of them. Indeed, why can't everyone be that way?

And even if some deep necessity requires that some or all of us hate to get out of bed, who is responsible for the fact that fish like to bite in the morning? Couldn't they have easily preferred mid-afternoon, so we could sleep in and still have a good day fishing?

And why does a fish's mouth have to be so hard to penetrate that a fishhook sharp enough to do its job poses a constant threat to an oaf like me?

Of course *my* answer to all of these questions is, "Well, that's just the breaks. No one decided all of this. It just worked out that way." But your answer is that God designed and created and thus bears responsibility for the whole thing.

Given this, how can you use the fishing analogy? It is designed to jolly me into believing in a "necessary evil"—something that is unpleasant or involves suffering, and so seems to be an evil, but turns out to be necessary for a greater good. But this analogy does no such thing. It is just an example of the very same thing I'm complaining about. I see no good reason a perfect being would want me to have the flu. And I see no good reason why a perfect being would want me to have to jerk myself out of bed with an unpleasant alarm in order to have a nice day fishing with a friend. The one evil does not explain the other; they both reinforce the same conclusion. No perfect God would have designed the world like this.

MILLER: You really know how to suffer, Gretchen. I can't believe you really expect my faith in God to be shaken by the fact that you have to get out of bed earlier than you would like to, to go fishing, or that when you are careless you prick your fingers with the fishhooks.

WEIROB: Keep in mind who has the burden of proof here. I don't have to talk you out of anything, nor do I want to. Believe what you want. You have to get me to believe, however, that your beliefs are consistent. I think you admit that I am suffering with this flu, however insignificant I may be in the grand scheme of things, and however inconsequential the flu may be in the great range of things people suffer. Yet you also think the world was created by a perfect God. I claim that those beliefs are inconsistent. The burden of proof is on you to show that they are not.

MILLER: But I think I have already done that. If the world consisted of only your suffering, and nothing else, it would certainly be a very poor world. And perhaps you even think of the world that way when you are not careful to keep your self-absorption in check. But the world does not consist of just you and your suffering. You and your suffering are part of a very big world, big spatially and in time, and perhaps in other dimensions we cannot fathom.

And it is consistent, I claim, that the events in this complex world are interconnected and interdependent in such a way that the world that contains them is a very wonderful place, and better because of your suffering than it would be without it.

WEIROB: But your analogy doesn't really show that. You tell me to think of a day when I went fishing and had a good day, even though the first part of it was unpleasant. I admit the day as a whole was good and well worth getting out of bed. But that isn't the point. Wouldn't the world have been better *without* my suffering? My suffering, my discomfort on rising early, detracted rather than added to the value of the day.

Similarly, I admit that this world, taken as a whole, including my suffering, may be a peachy keen world, just a humdinger of a world, a world any reasonably perfect deity might be proud of. But it seems to me that it would be obviously better if my suffering were removed. Everything good could be left behind. It might not make much difference to the world, but it seems like the world would definitely be a little bit better, and no worse. I don't see how the good parts of the world depend in any way on my suffering.

MILLER: No, that's not right. You suffer, as you say—I would say you are somewhat uncomfortable—whenever you get up at a reasonable hour. If the day had been without suffering, it would have been a day when you didn't get up early. But if you hadn't gotten up early, we would not have gone fishing together, because I left before dawn. Or you would have gone on your own, gotten to the river late, and returned home empty-handed. It would not have been much fun. If we subtract the suffering from the day, we subtract the early rising, and the successful fishing, and pretty much everything that made the day worthwhile. So your suffering did make the day better.

We can see, then, how the fineness of our fishing day did depend on your "suffering." Now how exactly the goodness of the world depends on your having the flu, I can't say. I can't trace the story as I did with our fishing day. But that's OK. I don't have to. I am simply trying to sort out the logic of the situation—that's all our little bet calls on me to do—even if the details are beyond my understanding.

WEIROB: But that returns us to the points I raised before. Granted, if we hold the dependencies fixed, my discomfort, as you refer to it, was a necessary condition of our successful fishing trip. But why should I hold the dependencies fixed? Aren't they due to your all-powerful God? To repeat the point, God could have made a world in which I loved to get out of bed—in which everyone did. Or he could have made a world in which the fish enjoyed sleeping until noon.

MILLER: I think I see your point. By the dependencies, you mean how one fact leads to another, the "if . . . then" statements, the general principles.

WEIROB: Yes, like "Normal people don't enjoy jumping out of bed at dawn" and "People who come into contact with such and such a microbe will turn into sniveling, dripping, headachy miserable wretches."

MILLER: The same principle applies. There is no inconsistency in supposing that a perfect God designed the world to work according to those principles, because having it work that way is necessary for some greater good.

WEIROB: Aren't those merely words? Can you really imagine what God might have had in mind that made my sniveling and sneezing and headaches necessary? It's very hard for me to imagine anything great and wonderful he couldn't have managed without my misery.

MILLER: But now you are making your imagination the test of God's existence. Why should we take what you can imagine—you, a finite, imperfect, middle-aged, drippy, sneezy, headachy, basically grouchy philosopher—to be a test of what might be the case?

Let me remind you of our deal. I don't have to explain to you what plan God has in mind, of which your rather insignificant drips and sneezes form a necessary part. I don't need to have a clue as to what it might be. I just have to show that it is consistent, logically consistent, not self-contradictory, for a perfect God to have created a world with some suffering. That I claim to have done, by showing that there is no contradiction in a perfect whole having parts that, considered by themselves, are quite imperfect.

Shall we pray?

WEIROB: Look, Sam, you are interspersing your philosophical arguments with some ad hominem attacks on me, as if I really believed that my sniveling and dripping were the worst thing God has ever done. But I certainly do not. I've just been trying to be polite to you and to your God, on the off chance that he or she exists.

But let me take my gloves off. My misery, though quite real and as far as I can see completely unnecessary and pointless, is small potatoes next to the things that have happened in this world that your supposedly all-perfect God has created. Just in our own century, there have been two world wars, countless smaller wars, mass murders, and so forth. Millions of people killed, soldiers ripped to pieces dying painful deaths, innocent children burned from napalm. There was the Holocaust, the systematic extermination of millions of Jews and others by the Nazis during World War II. There have been other genocides—and they don't all happen somewhere else, either. Columbus, Cortés, Pizarro—these great discoverers wiped out the Arawaks, the Aztecs, the Incas. Our nice little town and college on the prairie exist only because of the largely successful attempt to eliminate the Native Americans who dwelled here. And diseases much worse than the flu plague us—cancer, for example, which strikes so many people in the prime of their lives, often causes painful deaths and leaves grieving families. Will you just say glibly to these people that God must have a plan? It's all for the best? That their suffering, or that of their children or parents, is a necessary part of some plan of an all-perfect God? Is that what you say to grieving families on your pastoral visits?

MILLER: Yes, Gretchen, I do say that, or words to that effect. But I don't say it glibly. I say it quite humbly. And I don't say it because I think it will eliminate their grief. I say it because it leaves open the possibility that their loss might have some meaning.

And you know what, Gretchen? Most people don't feel the way you do. Most people are comforted by the idea of a design—even if it is completely unknown to us and impossible for us to imagine—that gives meaning to their suffering and loss. We know that for many, even in concentration camps, the conviction that, after all, their experience must somehow have some meaning, must fit into God's plan, was comforting, something to cling to.

So all of this evil, all of this suffering—to many of those who actually endure it—does not seem to be a knockdown refutation of the idea of a perfect God. I'm sure there are many like you who can't accept that a perfect God would find it necessary to inflict misery on them. But there are many others who accept their limitations, don't expect to understand what God has in mind, are grateful to know that a God who does have a plan exists. So, yes, I tell people who have suffered and are suffering just what you find so ridiculous. But most people don't find it ridiculous.

WEIROB: That was a passionate speech, Sam, and I guess it was in response to a tone of anger in mine.

I certainly admit that the phenomenon you have just described, the experience of seemingly pointless suffering driving people toward some faith in God, rather than, as I would think reasonable, away from it, is quite real. And not only real, but perhaps close to the heart of the religious impulse. So it might seem to be a paradox to argue that the very things that drive people to religion—suffering and evil—are in fact inconsistent with some of the religions to which they are driven—that is, the religions that believe in an all-perfect God.

It may *seem* like a paradox, but clearly no paradox exists.

MILLER: No, I suppose not. Your view, then, is this: the existence of suffering is inconsistent with the existence of the all-perfect God of orthodox Christianity, even though suffering, as much as anything, has led people to embrace Christianity. It is logically consistent, but it seems like a strange view.

WEIROB: I think I called your religion monstrous a minute ago, so I can't complain if you call my view strange.

But I see Dave coming up the walk. Let's break for lunch and see if we feel like continuing our discussion later.

MILLER: Are you ready for me to pray for you?

WEIROB: Not quite yet.

2

THE FIRST AFTERNOON

COHEN: That was a good lunch, Gretchen. Chicken soup is delicious, even for those of us without the flu.

WEIROB: I deserve some of the credit for buying the can. But Sam deserves most of it, for opening the can, adding the water, and heating it up.

MILLER: Not to mention Dave's putting out the bowls and spoons.

WEIROB: Right. Truly great cooking requires teamwork.

COHEN: I must say, however, that you two seemed lost in thought. I have the feeling you had quite a conversation before I got here. What's up?

MILLER: We were discussing the problem of evil. I made a bet with Gretchen. If I can show that there is nothing flatly and logically inconsistent about an all-perfect God creating a world with some evil in it, I win.

COHEN: And what is it you win?

MILLER: I get to say a prayer for her.

COHEN: Excuse me for saying so, but that doesn't seem like much to win. You can say a prayer for her any time you want. I'll bet you include her in your prayers every night.

MILLER: Yes, but in this case I will say it in her presence. She can't interrupt, or complain, or make fun of my beliefs. What's more, I'll say the prayer in the first person plural, that *we* pray for the salvation of her eternal soul.

WEIROB:　And that she get over the flu.

MILLER:　Right. I'll include that, too.

COHEN:　Well, who's winning?

MILLER:　I've already won; she just won't admit it. Now that you are here, Dave, you can be the judge. My basic position is quite straightforward. An object or event can contain parts that, considered by themselves, lack whatever kind of goodness we might be talking about. And yet the presence of these parts can contribute to the overall goodness of the whole object. A painting can have ugly parts but be more <u>beautiful</u> or aesthetically pleasing or deep because of them. A symphony can have discordant notes and be better, as a whole, for it. A day can be a fine day, a perfect day, even though it contains a little suffering—say, that goes with getting up at the break of dawn. So, for all Gretchen knows, God may have a plan in which the suffering in the world plays an important role in making the whole better than it would be otherwise. Of particular interest to her, of course, is the intense and nearly unbearable suffering she is enduring as a result of her flu, although she admits that there are some other cases worthy of mention. I may not be able to say what God's plan is—why should a limited creature like myself be capable of that?—but I think I can claim to have shown that it is consistent to suppose that this world is the creation of an all-perfect Being, even if we admit that there is suffering in it.

COHEN:　That sounds pretty good. What is your problem with that, Gretchen?

WEIROB: First of all, let me utterly disavow the mean
            suggestion Sam has made that I give my own
            sniveling and dripping some special status. I
            not only mention, I emphasize, that there have
            been events in this world, and no doubt these
            events are occurring this very minute, that are
            many orders of magnitude worse cases of suf-
            fering than my flu. So much the worse for Sam's
            argument. The worse the evil, the bigger the
            problem.
                Second, let me explain why I don't think Sam
            has won yet. The deal was that he was to show
            me a possibility. That is, he was to show me how
            it was possible that a world with evil in it, the
            kind of evil we see here on earth, could be the
            creation of a perfect God.
                Here's the way I see it. We have two state-
            ments, call them P and Q.

MILLER: Uh-oh. I hope you aren't going to get technical
            and try to win a philosophical argument with an
            equation.

WEIROB: No, nothing like that. Nothing at all. Just a sim-
            ple point. So you've got two statements, P and
            Q. You think they are consistent, that is, that
            both could be true. I think they aren't consis-
            tent; that is, I don't see how they could both be
            true. But I admit that they are not *explicitly*
            inconsistent. P and Q aren't like "It's raining"
            and "It's not raining." Q isn't simply the nega-
            tion of P.

COHEN: In this case P is that a perfect God exists, and Q
            is that all this evil we observe occurs.

WEIROB: Right. Now what does someone have to do to
            convince me that P and Q are consistent? They
            need to describe a bigger picture into which

they both fit, a bigger picture that is itself clearly consistent.

MILLER: I thought that was what I was doing. Perhaps you could give an example of what would satisfy you.

WEIROB: I can give a simple example. Suppose I claim that there is a barber who shaves all and only those residents of Wilbur who do not shave themselves. Let me make the point a little more explicit. There are two things true about this barber. Call the first P: he shaves all the residents of Wilbur who don't shave themselves. Call the second Q: he doesn't shave anyone else. Would you say that was possible?

MILLER: I'd say it's impossible. There could not be such a barber. He would either shave himself or not. But either choice leads to a blatant contradiction. If he shaves himself, then he shaves someone who shaves himself, which contradicts his description. If he doesn't shave himself, then he doesn't shave someone who doesn't shave himself, contrary to his description. So there can't be such a barber. He is like a thing that is both round and square. You can describe such a thing but there can't be such a thing. The description "the barber who shaves all and only the people who don't shave themselves" can't fit anything.

WEIROB: But remember, I didn't say "all and only the people," I said, "all and only the residents of Wilbur."

COHEN: Right! OK, I get it. The barber lives in Beatrice, where his partner shaves him. Every day he drives to Wilbur and shaves all the residents who don't shave themselves. No contradiction.

MILLER: Tricky, tricky.

WEIROB: The point is that something *seemed* contradic-
            tory. But it really wasn't. This was shown by
            constructing a bigger picture that made sense
            out of how P and Q could both be true.

            The bigger picture did not need to be *true* in
            order to do the trick of showing that P and Q are
            consistent. Maybe the barber actually lives in
            Crete and not in Beatrice. Or maybe he lives on
            a farm and has a beard. Or whatever. The bigger
            picture just has to be clearly consistent. It has to
            do what Dave did: show us that we were assum-
            ing something that made P and Q seem incon-
            sistent, but that actually they could be fit
            together.

MILLER: But Gretchen, isn't that precisely what I have
            been doing? I even used the words, "big pic-
            ture." I've been saying there is a big picture, and
            if we could only see it, we could see how the
            sufferings in the world contribute to the good-
            ness of the world taken as a whole. You admit I
            don't have to actually tell you what the big pic-
            ture is.

WEIROB: I don't think you give me what I have a right to
            ask for. Suppose Dave had just said, "I don't
            think that the barber is impossible because, for
            all we know, there is some larger story that
            makes it all fit together." That wouldn't have
            convinced you, would it?

MILLER: No, certainly not.

            So let me see if I've got your point. Could we
            put it like this: what is needed is not just the
            possibility of providing a big picture, but an
            actual providing of a possible big picture.

WEIROB: Yes, that's it exactly. You can't get by just assert-
ing that there might be some big plan into
which everything fits. On the other hand, you
aren't required to come up with the true big picture, any more than Dave had to tell us where
the barber actually lives. You need to do something in between. As you put it, you need to
actually provide me with a story that makes
God's perfection and the suffering of his creatures fit together in a consistent whole. The
whole need not be true. It can be far-fetched
and unbelievable. And of course we agreed that
you didn't have to provide details accounting
for every evil we can think of. But you need to
show how evil can enter into a world created by
your all-perfect God, to show the basic mechanisms of evil, one might say.

COHEN: That seems reasonable, Sam. Can you do that?

MILLER: I think I can. Let me make sure that I have the
ground rules straight. My story has to show that
such a world—that is, a world with the sorts of
suffering and evil we have in this one, and created by an all-powerful, knowing, and benevolent God—is logically possible. To do this I need
to construct a story of how things might be in a
way that explains the suffering and evil as parts
in a perfect world. That I think I can do. But I
want to warn you at the outset, the story will
contain elements that Gretchen—and no doubt
you, too, Dave—will find completely unbelievable. But you won't, I think, claim that they are
contradictory, and that's what counts. Are we
now agreed on the ground rules?

COHEN: I think so. You will describe a consistent world
that contains the suffering and evil the real
world contains and is created by an all-perfect
God. The world can contain any events you

want, however unlikely Gretchen thinks they may be, as long as they are consistent. If you do that, you will show that it is possible, at least in the logical sense of not containing any contradictions, that our world, with all the kinds of suffering and evil Gretchen has mentioned, was created by a God such as you believe in. Do you agree to that, Gretchen?

WEIROB: Yes, I agree. I don't think I'm going to particularly like what is coming, but I agree that if Sam can describe such a world, however implausible I may find it, he will have won the bet.

MILLER: Frankly, that's very good news. There is a traditional story, a sort of Christian theodicy. It has three parts, and I'm sure that you guys won't think that the last two parts are at all plausible. But under these rules you don't have to find them plausible. As long as you find them possible, I win.

COHEN: Theodicy. What's a theodicy?

WEIROB: Leibniz wrote a book called *Theodicy,* which is his account of how this is the best of all possible worlds, contrary to appearances. Sort of an apology for God. These are the ideas Voltaire makes fun of in *Candide,* the ideas that Dr. Pangloss defends. So I suppose that a theodicy is an apology for God for making such a dismal world.

MILLER: I wouldn't put it quite like that, although I suppose one might. A theodicy is just the sort of thing you want me to provide. But there are things Leibniz wanted to prove that I'm not going to attempt. First, to repeat once more, I don't have to claim that the possibility I'm describing is correct about the real world, just that it is a possibility. Second, I don't see why I should show that this is the best of all possible worlds. I don't see why we should assume that there would be a unique best world. And finally—I guess this is a separate point—if there were a best of all possible worlds, I might not be in it. I'm not going to get upset with God for not making a world I'm not in. I don't see why you have any valid complaint that God didn't make a world that you are not in.

WEIROB: I'm not so sure about that last point, but let's let it pass, at least for now.

MILLER: The first thing I need to explain—the first thing in my theodicy, I guess I should say—seems to be something you won't find so implausible. That is the idea that a world with freedom in it is better than one without freedom.

COHEN: You probably don't mean things like freedom of religion, freedom of speech, freedom of assembly, the sorts of things that are guaranteed in America by the Bill of Rights. You mean something more basic and metaphysical.

MILLER: That's right. All of those freedoms are wonderful. But they presuppose freedom in a more basic sense. They presuppose freedom of choice. The choice may be dramatic, such as when one is deciding whether to publish something unpopular or whether to assemble to protest an unjust law. But there is choice involved even when the choice is fairly trivial. For example, Gretchen had a can of mushroom soup and a can of chicken soup in her pantry. I asked her which she wanted me to fix, and she decided on chicken soup. There wasn't anything momentous about this decision. Probably even in the most vicious tyranny, people would be allowed to choose between chicken soup and mushroom soup. But the point is, she had to choose. She decided. The response that she made when she chose chicken soup wasn't automatic. She thought it over, she deliberated, however briefly, on which she would enjoy more, and she chose. She could have chosen one way or the other; she chose chicken. That is freedom of choice in the sense that I mean.

WEIROB: So you're saying that a world with creatures like us, who have this ability to choose between different courses of action, is better than one without creatures like us in that respect. I suppose that might be a world in which there was nothing but robots, whose every act was programmed in a predictable way.

MILLER: That's right. Withhold your disbelief for a second, and imagine being God, or at least a very powerful creator, who is going to create a world. Wouldn't it be a good thing to create creatures that have freedom?

WEIROB: What would be so good about it?

MILLER: Gretchen, I know you can simply throw up doubts at every step of my argument, but what kind of discussion will we have then? You need to let me explain my vision—the defense to the problem of evil, as I understand it. I think you grasp what I'm getting at. Remember, I don't claim to understand the world. As a Christian who believes in an all-perfect God, I don't expect to. I don't expect to understand the mind of an infinite God.

WEIROB: I don't either; I can't even understand the mind of the person who wrote the instruction book for my VCR.

MILLER: My task is only to provide one story of how things *might* all fit together. All I'm really trying to say is that we can admit that an all-perfect God *might* have valued that trait of ours that we call freedom of choice. Such a God might have preferred to create a world with such creatures in it to one that was like it in other ways, but contained only automatons or robots.

WEIROB: OK, I'll give you that for now. But I want to reserve the right to return later to this picture you have of the difference between us and automatons and robots.

COHEN: But for now we all admit that it's quite coherent to suppose an all-perfect creator who preferred (in whatever ways all-perfect beings do) to create a world with free creatures than one without such creatures. What's the next step?

MILLER: In creating such a world, the creator then takes a certain amount of risk. God gives up control of every facet of the universe. If he creates Gretchen with free will, then whether Gretchen takes the chicken soup or the mushroom soup is up to her, not to God. That's the meaning of free choice.

Of course, this decision is not of much importance. At least as far as we can see, it wasn't right to choose chicken and wrong to choose mushroom, or vice versa. It's just a matter of what she felt like having.

But many of the decisions free creatures make, many of the decisions we make, are not like that. Often we are faced with a decision between something that is right and something that is wrong. Or between something that is OK and something that is noble.

In these cases there is no question of what God would have us do. God would have us do

what is better, and more noble, and more perfect. But what we do is up to us. And we don't
always do the right instead of the wrong, the
better rather than worse, the noble over the
merely sufficient. In this way, through the
actions of humans and other free creatures exercising their freedom, imperfection and evil enter
the world.

Suppose we are at a picnic, and we drink a
six-pack of pop that came from the store with
one of those plastic bridles that holds the cans
together. You know that birds and other animals
can get caught in the holes in those things and
end up dying an agonizing death because they
can't eat properly, and so they slowly starve.
Suppose one of those bridles blows away. We
could chase it down, but we don't. Perhaps we
even intend to do so later, and then forget. So
our wrong is merely a bit of procrastination. Not
such a big deal. But later a bird gets caught in
the holes and suffers a painful death. The bird's
suffering was real. It wasn't something God
chose. Nor even something we chose directly.
But it was our choice not to do what we knew
was right, to take a chance on what would happen with the plastic bridle.

Here, then, is something quite bad in our
world, something we cannot imagine God
choosing. The explanation is that it isn't his
choice to have the bird suffer. His role is to
make us free. He must value freedom so much
that all the bad results that come from the decisions creatures freely make, still leave it a better world, in his eyes, than one without free
creatures.

That seems to me the basic story that
Augustine and others tell to explain how evil
enters the world. I know it's a rather trivial
example, and perhaps the suffering of one bird
is nothing compared to the suffering of millions

of children over the centuries. But it illustrates what we might call the basic mechanism of evil in a world created by perfection.

COHEN: Gretchen, are you satisfied so far?

WEIROB: Not exactly. I have a couple of questions.

Let's suppose, as would probably be the case, that I am the culprit in your little story. That is, I leave the plastic bridle unsecured on the beach, I see it blow away, I resolve to get it but procrastinate and then forget. The key point is when I decide—freely—to bask in the sun for a few minutes before going to get it. I could do either thing. I could do the right thing and run right after the bridle. Or I could do what I did in fact do, and just sit there and enjoy the sun and the conversation, running the risk of forgetting all about it. And that's what I did.

Now I can agree with you that an all-perfect God might want to populate the world with free creatures. But why does he want to populate it with *lazy* free creatures, like me? If I hadn't been lazy, I would have shot up and gotten the bridle right away. I would still have been free, just not lazy. Couldn't God have created a world with free creatures, but free creatures that have no relevant weaknesses, so that they always freely choose to do the right thing? Then evil wouldn't have crept into the world.

MILLER: I'm certainly not going to deny that you are lazy, or that laziness is by any reasonable standard an imperfection. To stick with the example, why did God make a lazy Gretchen rather than a perfect Gretchen?

COHEN: No, that's not the point; Gretchen isn't claiming that her only imperfection is laziness. But it seems that she would be a better person if she weren't lazy, even if everything else stayed the same.

MILLER: Now you are trying to get me to give some sort of detailed account of what God had in mind by creating a world in which Gretchen is lazy. And of course if I could do that, you would move on to other people and other, worse problems. You would ask me to explain what God had in mind in creating a world in which Hitler exists with all of his hatred, and so forth. But remember our agreement. I don't have to do that. I don't claim to be able to explain in any detail what God is aiming at. I just want to explain how there are certain basic mechanisms that allow us to see how God could create a world in which bad things are done.

I may not be able to think of any good purpose that is promoted by Gretchen's laziness. I must admit it would seem to me to be a better world if she had all of her other charms—most of them, anyway—but wasn't lazy. But how should I know? How should my tiny mind figure out what purpose Gretchen's laziness serves?

In any case, if you look at the example, you must admit that the bird's suffering was Gretchen's fault, not God's. Gretchen *could have* picked up the bridle. She chose not to. She was free. And so she, and not someone else, not God, is responsible for the consequences of her actions.

COHEN: Wait a minute, don't you Christians think she really *wasn't* free? Don't you hold that without intervention by God, without God's grace, without a little mysterious infusion of willpower, she could not have chosen to do the good?

WEIROB: Sam is just being considerate by leaving out the doctrine of grace. I told him that explanations of

the concept of grace first make me dizzy, then
give me a headache.

MILLER: I didn't promise not to discuss it. There certainly
is that wrinkle in many versions of Christianity,
including mine, as a good Presbyterian. Adam
was the last human to have complete free will
to choose the good; since then, we have had no
free will without God's grace. But I think we can
probably set that aside. If I can't convince
Gretchen of the straightforward free will
defense of God, the doctrine of grace won't
help me. If I can convince her of that much,
maybe I'll make a try at grace.

WEIROB: Isn't God supposed to give us grace if we ask?

MILLER: I wouldn't want to tell God what he is supposed
to do, but, yes, most Christians believe that, in
fact, if we ask, we will receive—I think those
are the words Augustine used. . . .

WEIROB: No, no, spare me the details. I think we can just
ignore grace. My point is this. Let's stipulate that
we are always free to ask for God's help to do A,
for any good action A. And that, if we ask, we'll
get his help, and then we will have freedom to
do A. So it won't get me off the hook to claim
that, because of God and Adam, I wasn't really
free not to be lazy and pick up the bridle. I was
free to ask for God's help, and if I had done that,
I would have been free to pick up the bridle
without delay. As far as I can see, our lack of
free will to choose the good is canceled by our
guarantee of God's grace, which would be
pretty hollow if we weren't free to choose at
least that. The whole business of God's grace
just sort of cancels the limits on our free will.

Sam, I'm sure this is oversimple and doesn't
get at your deep feelings about grace. The most

amazing thing about grace, as far as I can see, is that anyone dreamed it up.

MILLER: Oh, Gretchen, it's such a beautiful concept. And the song is beautiful too.

WEIROB: I'll go part of the way with you. The song "Amazing Grace" is indeed very beautiful, and I'm sure the emotions that inspired it were profound. But the concept itself—well, I just don't get it. I hate to spend the rest of the afternoon discussing it. So I'll stipulate that Sam doesn't have to defend that peculiar wrinkle. We can all be Pelagians this afternoon, and suppose that we are all as free as Adam. If Sam can make this miserable world a plausible creation of an all-perfect Pelagian God, given that assumption, he wins.

COHEN: Forgive my ignorance of the details of your somewhat convoluted offshoot of *my* religion, but what exactly are you talking about, "We can all be Pelagians"?

MILLER: Pelagius was a British monk, a contemporary of Augustine, who thought Augustine's way of thinking about original sin, free will, and grace was confused. In Pelagius' view we have free will, the power to do the right thing, without any special dispensation from God. In Augustine's view, that was only true of Adam. Grace, according to Pelagius, was not God's giving us the power to do right, but God's rewarding us for doing right. I daresay the average Christian these days is closer to Pelagius' heresy than to Augustine's orthodoxy on these issues, without knowing it.

COHEN: It sounds like we should be Pelagians for this discussion, if we want to keep it philosophical.

WEIROB: So let's do that. Go ahead, Sam. Show us why a
           Pelagian God is a plausible creator of this mis-
           erable world.

MILLER: Hold on, Gretchen. Not *plausible,* just *consis-
           tent.* That was our deal.

WEIROB: OK, OK.
           But is your view really consistent? After all,
           your God is supposed to be omniscient, all-
           knowing. Ignorance would clearly be an imper-
           fection.
               If God is all-knowing, doesn't that mean he
           must know what each of us will do next?
           Doesn't he know that I will choose the chicken,
           not the mushroom, soup? Doesn't he know that
           I will let the bridle lie where it landed? If so,
           how can I be free? If not, if he doesn't know
           what I am going to do, then how can he be
           omniscient?

COHEN: I don't think that quite follows, Gretchen.
           Suppose Sam asks you if you would rather have
           a spinach soufflé or a T-bone steak for dinner. I
           know you would choose the steak. You might
           hesitate, thinking that the soufflé would be
           more healthy, that perhaps there are good argu-
           ments against eating animals. But you'd take the
           steak. You like steak so much and spinach so lit-
           tle, that anyone who knows you would predict
           it. I know that about as well as I know that the
           sun will rise tomorrow. But that doesn't mean
           that you didn't choose the steak freely, does it?
           You chose the steak because you wanted to. You
           knew the spinach would be better for you, but
           you chose the steak, as free as can be. My
           knowledge or lack of knowledge has nothing to
           do with it.

MILLER: Good point, Dave.

WEIROB: I admit that Dave's point is good. It doesn't fol-
low from the fact that Dave knows what I will
choose, that I don't choose freely. So Sam isn't
consistent, simply because he says that I am
free, and that someone knows what I am going
to do.

Still, Sam doesn't just say that, he says that
the someone is God—the very same God who
created me. And it seems that God hasn't figured out what I am like, after long experience,
as you two have. He knew from the moment he
created me, or before, precisely what I would
do, from my first cry on being born to my dying
utterance. Given that, I don't understand exactly
how he can escape responsibility for what I do.

God's knowledge is a special case. He created me, knowing what I would do. You didn't
create me. You didn't decide on a plan for the
world that involved my eating the steak. If we
trace back from effect to cause, starting with my
choosing the steak, we will not come to you as
a distant cause of my action. That's why I am
responsible for eating the steak and you are not.
But the situation is completely different with
God. If we trace back from effect to cause, we
do come to God as a distant cause. So God
doesn't escape responsibility for the consequences of what I do, since they are part of the
consequences, for him the *foreseeable* consequences, of what he did.

It seems ludicrous to have someone create a
situation that he knows, prior to creation, will
lead to an unfortunate result, blame the result
on some aspect of the situation he created—in
this case, me—and avoid any responsibility at
all for it. It makes me . . .

MILLER: Wait a minute, Gretchen. You're getting off the
point and forgetting your own train of thought.

There are two points here. The one you have drifted into now is this: Does God's knowledge of what you will do, given that he created you, mean that God bears some responsibility for what you do? I must admit it seems pretty plausible that it does mean this. But that has nothing to do with our argument at this point. I haven't said that God isn't responsible for everything that happens in his creation. I've just said that things that seem unnecessary and bad might be necessary parts of a good or even perfect world.

The second point is this: Does God's knowledge of what you are going to do mean that *you are not free after all?* That question is relevant to our discussion at this point. You were claiming that what I said was inconsistent, that an omniscient God could not make people who were truly free, since if he is omniscient, he'll know what they are going to choose.

Dave pointed out that in at least some cases, someone can know that a person will do a certain thing, even though the person does that thing freely. His example was that though he knows you will choose steak, your choice is still a free choice.

WEIROB: Sam, you're exactly right. I was getting off on another point.

Let's see, can God create someone who is free, and at the same time know what he or she is going to do? I think I still have some difficulty with that, even when I am not confused.

But to tell you the truth, between your subtleties and my flu, my intellect is beginning to show signs of wear and tear. If I were to suggest we pick up on this tomorrow morning, Sam, would you feel I was just trying to wangle another cinnamon roll out of you?

MILLER: Of course not. And tomorrow I'll try to do a better job explaining how we can be free, even if
God created us knowing what choices we
would make.
    I'll pick up a roll for you too, Dave, if you can
make it.

COHEN: Count me in for sure. I'm anxious to hear the
next part of your "big picture." What time?

MILLER: My reasoning this morning went like this:
Gretchen and I belong to a generation that
thinks breakfast at eight is getting pretty late.
Add an hour for Gretchen's laziness, which we
have commented on so much. Add another
hour because she has the flu. Ten o'clock
seemed to be just about perfect.

WEIROB: Yes, it was, and it will be. See you guys then. I'll
even brew the coffee, Sam, just bring the rolls
and the rest of your big picture.

3

THE SECOND MORNING

WEIROB: Good morning, Sam. Those rolls look good. And here is Dave, just coming up the walk.

COHEN: Good morning, Sam. Good morning, Gretchen. Wow, coffee, cinnamon rolls, and philosophy. What a great way to start the day! Sam, you look sort of glum.

MILLER: I have to admit I am a bit discouraged. What I wanted to do today was to explain to you two how God can be omniscient—he knows everything the creatures he creates are going to do— and still give them free choice.

I thought I'd be able to do this by simply reviewing what some of my heroes have said, particularly Augustine. So I stayed up pretty late reading and thinking. But to tell you the truth, I don't really find a solution there that I feel is convincing. I'm sure the problem is with me and not with Augustine, but I can't very well explain what I wanted to explain.

WEIROB: What does Augustine *say?*

MILLER: He makes Dave's point, that there is no contradiction between your being free and someone knowing what you are going to do next. We might know you will choose the steak rather than the spinach soufflé, but that doesn't mean your choice isn't free. But he doesn't go much further than that. He doesn't seem to feel it makes a difference in the case in which it is the creator that knows what the created is going to do. To be honest, I can't get away from thinking it does make a difference. I'm not really sure that it makes sense for me to be free, when the very person who created me knew that if he created me one way, I would do the one thing, and if he created me another way, I would do the other. And, even if that does make sense, it seems that it is clearly God who is choosing the evil that we do. He is doing it at one remove: he is choosing to make someone who will choose to do the evil. I can't really convince myself that this makes much of a difference. So I'm stuck. I don't really think the problem is unsolvable, but *I* don't know how to solve it.

COHEN: I don't want to be presumptuous—as a matter of fact, I don't even know which side I'm on in your debate. But I thought a lot about this God and free will problem last night, and I'd like to try out an idea on you two.

MILLER: Be my guest!

COHEN: Let me start with another problem, which we studied in a philosophy class I took a long time ago.

MILLER: *Another problem?* Are you sure you are trying to help?

COHEN: Just hang on. I think it's a *solvable* problem, and that the solution suggests an idea about the free will problem.

MILLER: OK.

COHEN: The problem is called "The Stone Paradox." It's an objection to God's omnipotence. You ask the question, "Could God create a stone he could not lift?" That question is supposed to pose a paradox that shows that the idea of God's

omnipotence makes no sense. If God can't create the stone, there is something he can't do.
But if he can create the stone, there is something he can't do, namely, lift the stone he created. Either way, there is something God can't
do, which proves he isn't omnipotent after all.

WEIROB: I've always thought that was a pretty nifty problem for theists. But I guess you think it doesn't
hold up.

COHEN: No, I don't. When we say that God is omnipotent, we mean God can perform any act or task
that makes sense. We don't mean that God can
make something that is both round and square,
or can make two and two add up to five, or anything like that. But "create a stone God cannot
lift" is itself an impossible, incoherent task, if
God is essentially omnipotent. It doesn't make
sense for anyone to perform this task. Therefore
it doesn't make sense for God to. It's not really
a task.

WEIROB: OK, that's pretty convincing. What does that
have to do with the problem about God and
free will?

COHEN: Hold on a minute. I've got another point. Notice
that God in fact created all sorts of stones that
he *will* not in fact lift—I'm not really sure what
it means for God to lift a stone, but whatever we
take it to mean, my point holds.

MILLER: Granted. Go ahead and explain it.

COHEN: OK. Take the Rock of Gibraltar. Suppose that for
God to lift a stone means that he miraculously
makes it rise for no apparent reason and then
settle softly back where it was. God has a plan
for the world, and in that plan he simply does

not perform that act. He does not lift the Rock of Gibraltar.

WEIROB: OK, OK. What's the point?

COHEN: Just that God *can* lift the Rock of Gibraltar, in the sense that *if* he had planned the world that way, that's what would have happened. I don't know what else it would mean, to say that God could lift it, if it weren't that. It isn't that it's too big or heavy for him. He won't lift it, but he could. And "he could" means that he could have created a world in which he did.

WEIROB: All right. God won't lift the Rock of Gibraltar, because he decided not to. But he could lift it, because if that's what he had decided to do, that's what he would have done.

COHEN: Let's take seriously the idea that God decides to create a world with free agents. And let's accept that part of deciding this is that he is not going to know what these agents will do at certain points in their lives. Note that this is not to say that God *cannot* know. It is that he has decided *not* to know. He could have created a world in which he knew whether Gretchen would pick up the soda bridle right away, or whether she would decide to wait. So he could know. But he doesn't know.

WEIROB: But if God doesn't know which I'm going to do, is God really omniscient?

COHEN: It seems to me that, in a pretty clear and defensible sense, God *is* omniscient in the case I am describing. Remember, he is *omnipotent* not because he *does* everything there is to be done, but because there is nothing he can't *do*. He is *omniscient* not because he knows everything, but because there is nothing that he can't *know.*

MILLER: This is sounding pretty good to me, though I'm not too sure what Augustine would say about it. However, I'm not certain we can accept so lenient a concept of omniscience as this. I mean, God is supposed to know quite a bit, after all. If I understand your definition, he might not know anything and still be omniscient, as long as there is nothing he could not have known had he wanted to.

COHEN: Maybe my definition of omniscience isn't quite right. Perhaps I'll come back to that later. My main point is a bit different. Look at all that God does know, from this perspective. God can still know all the principles and laws by which the world works—which of course we imagine being due to God. He may not know whether Gretchen will choose the mushroom soup or the chicken soup, but he knows just what will happen if she does the one or the other.

MILLER: How is *that* knowledge about the world?

COHEN: God's picture of the world is like a road map of Nebraska. Suppose we look at a road map, and imagine a driver entering the state from Kansas on Highway 75.

MILLER: Driving up from Topeka?

WEIROB: I don't think it really matters, Sam.

MILLER: I know that, Gretchen. I just like to have a vivid picture in my imagination.

COHEN: Then let's say driving up from Topeka. So he has lots of points at which to choose. When he comes to Nebraska City, he can take Highway 2. That will take him toward Lincoln, and if he stays on it until the end . . .

WEIROB: The bitter end, if it's winter.

COHEN: . . . he'll come to Chadron. If he stays on Highway 85, he'll head toward Omaha, and if he continues to stay on 85, he'll eventually come to Sioux City, I guess. My point is that we know quite a bit about the driver. Even if we don't know the choices he will make, we know the *consequences* of each choice.

WEIROB: Of course, the consequence of each choice will not be a fixed route through the rest of the state, but another set of choices—that's not an objection, just a comment.

COHEN: Just add one thing: suppose that we are not merely looking at a regular road map, but at an electronic road map that has a little light on it that follows the progress of the car. What's more, suppose that we have a radio control device that allows us to take over the steering of the car. At any intersection, we could decide which way the car will go, and so we could know which way the car will go. But we decide not to do that.

In this case, it seems to me we could know everything about the car's route through the state, for we could have a plan in which we use the car's radio control to go in a predetermined way at each intersection. But we ourselves choose to let the driver decide, at least at some of the intersections. We could know, but we ourselves decided not to know. We know everything that can be known, given our decision. And even in this case, we know all the effects of each of the free "choices"—although, as

Gretchen pointed out, this knowledge is full of ifs: "if he turns on 2, then if he doesn't turn off on 77 or 30 or the interstate . . . then he will arrive in Chadron, but if he turns left on 77, he will end up in Beatrice"—and so forth. This sort of knowledge is hard to put into words, but a map represents it very elegantly.

But to return to the point, we can know everything; we do in fact know a lot, and the things we don't know are the things we decided not to know.

It seems this might be an acceptable model for Sam. If it works, it allows for a God who can know everything and does in fact know everything, except the things he has chosen not to know, by virtue of giving free choice to humans.

WEIROB: To improve the model, you should give us not just the knowledge of the way the roads go in Nebraska, but the ability to design and build them ourselves. We decided where the roads would go, and so we decided what the effects of the choices would be.

MILLER: Fair enough. If I understand Dave, this is the idea. First, think of God's knowledge as a big diagram of all the events that are going to happen through time. Next to each time on the diagram is written the state of the world at that specific time. Think of God deliberating, and then choosing between an infinity of these diagrams—choosing one and saying, "So Be It," or something like that. (Of course, theologians will tell us that that is not an accurate way to conceive of how God knows, since it is based on how we know. But still, it's a useful way of thinking about it.)

According to Dave's conception, we shouldn't think of these diagrams simply as time lines with descriptions of the world attached at each time. Rather, each diagram has many branches. For each time a free being is faced with a choice, the diagram will have a fork, with one branch representing how the world will go on if the person makes one decision and the other branch representing how the world will proceed if the person makes another decision.

WEIROB: Of course a person might have several choices, so that this fork might have a number of branches coming out of it.

MILLER: Right. This diagram would quickly become enormously complex. If we just think of five people making decisions every five minutes, the representation of all the ways things might go would be too complex for any human to deal with before an hour had passed.

WEIROB: I've read, though, that this is how chess-playing computers work. They form a big picture of all the ways the game can continue from a given position—or at least an enormous number of positions—and figure out from that what the best move is. It's clear that that is not the way humans play chess.

MILLER: Well, I'm sure that neither is a very good model for how God plans things, and probably even to talk about planning is misleading. But this way of looking at it, even though it makes God sound like a chess-playing computer to you, Gretchen, is the way I picture what Dave's suggestion amounts to.

I think I like it. God decides the range of choices to give people, the way the world works, the effects of the various decisions, including how they frame later decisions. However, he decides to put an element of free choice in. As Dave says, he could have known what people will do at those points, but he chooses not to. God is still omniscient in the sense that he *can* know everything, in the sense Dave explains, and he *does* know everything that doesn't turn on free choices.

WEIROB: Are you sure that this concept of omniscience will pass muster with expert theologians, like our hero Augustine?

COHEN: Augustine is your hero? Isn't he supposed to be responsible for a lot of the uptightness that infects Christianity?

WEIROB: Well, I don't admire him for that, but I do think he was a great philosopher, even though I've only read bits and pieces.

MILLER: You ask whether he would approve of this concept of omniscience. I really don't know if he would, Gretchen. It certainly doesn't seem to be the concept he used, so I suppose he wouldn't like it.

But if you are thinking of that as an excuse to wiggle out of admitting that you have lost the bet, think again. You don't accept anyone's authority on anything, and you can't start now by appealing to the authority of Augustine. If you yourself can't come up with a good reason not to accept Dave's account of our freedom and God's knowledge, you lose. Ready for a prayer?

WEIROB: Oh, no. You've got a long way to go. I'll give you freedom. Although I'm not completely convinced, I just don't have any good arguments to show that Dave's account is inconsistent or incoherent.

Where does that leave us? You've given us a God that is perfect, that thinks a world with freedom is better than one without, even if that means that if some choices are made, suffering will result.

So let's look at our world with this in mind. The first thing to note is that there is a lot of suffering. But you say that is the result of free choices by free beings; their freedom was the price God was willing to pay for a world with free beings.

But isn't your God also supposed to be a just and fair God? Doesn't this require that those who suffer have this suffering balanced by pleasure or even joy? And doesn't it require that those who cause the suffering—at least those who choose to do evil or, like me in the case of the soda bridle, choose to be lazy and thoughtless—should be punished? But who can look around the world and suppose that there is this kind of justice and fairness? You may have explained how a perfect God can end up creating a world with suffering, but I don't see how you have explained how he can end up creating a world that is as unfair and unjust as ours.

COHEN: I'm pretty sure I know what Sam is going to say about that, Gretchen.

WEIROB: I think I do too, but I want to hear him say it.

MILLER: I told you yesterday my theodicy has three parts, and I said the first part, freedom, was the one you would probably like best.

The second part is one of the most familiar and, I think, also one of the most beautiful ideas that people associate with religion in general and Christianity in particular. That is the notion of an afterlife.

WEIROB: Heaven, hell, and I suppose purgatory, too.

MILLER: Those are parts of Dante's picture. But I don't have to buy into any details. The point is simply this. Suppose an innocent child is run over by a car, suffers, and eventually dies. The driver was criminally negligent, but rich. His only real punishment is the high fees he must pay to his lawyer. The child dies after a life in which the suffering outweighs the joys; the driver has a pleasant life. If we have only this to go on, how can we say that ours is a just world?

But the doctrine of an afterlife, in whatever form, says that this isn't the whole story. The driver may have a very unpleasant afterlife. If we think in traditional terms, we may imagine him suffering in purgatory for a long time, or perhaps even being given everlasting torment in hell. But we don't have to have anything like Dante's version of the afterlife to grasp the general point. If the part of the world we see is all there is, God has clearly created a very unfair and unjust world. But there is no inconsistency—and let me remind you, I don't have to convince you of the plausibility of my story, of my theodicy, only that it is consistent and coherent—in claiming that what we see is not all there is, and that the sufferings are compensated for and the sins are punished in parts of existence of which we cannot now be aware.

WEIROB: I think this whole issue of the afterlife is an interesting one. I can imagine there is a place far away in space and time, or perhaps far away in another dimension I don't even have a concept of, in which someone is suffering because I was careless with the soda bridle. But unless that person is me, it just makes the whole world more unfair. And what would make her me? That's what bothers me. I wonder if that whole idea isn't pretty dubious.

COHEN: That's a pretty subtle point. Are we going to have to figure out the nature of personal identity and immortality before we know whether Sam has won his bet?

MILLER: I don't think that's quite fair, Gretchen. Life after death may not be common sense; maybe it's completely fantastic, as I'm sure you must think. But the *possibility* of life after death is common sense; everyone knows what we mean when we say we might end up in heaven or hell, or be reincarnated. I can't be expected to solve every philosophy problem there is, can I?

WEIROB: All right, all right. I'm sure we'll get around to talking about that topic some day. But for now I'll drop it. I'll give you the possibility of an afterlife, and with it the possibility that your God is just and fair, appearances to the contrary.

MILLER: Well, I guess I should thank you for permitting me to embrace a concept that has given hope and meaning to countless souls throughout the centuries.

WEIROB: You are very welcome. My generosity knows bounds, however. I think there is a bigger problem. Indeed, it makes me feel bad just to think of it, and to remember our casual talk about fishing yesterday. After all, animals suffer too. You have to get your God off the hook for that.

COHEN: I suppose Sam can say that animals suffer because of someone's free choice, and the suffering can be compensated for in an afterlife.

WEIROB: No, I think the problem goes quite a bit deeper than that. Hold on, let me get the copy of *Natural History* magazine that I was reading. . . . It's got to be in that pile over there. . . .

Here it is. Now, look at the picture on the inside of the back cover.

MILLER: Oh, dear.

COHEN: I can't quite make it out. What is it?

WEIROB: Do you know what a bat cave is?

MILLER: Of course.

COHEN: I'm afraid you are going to have to explain it to this city boy.

WEIROB: A bat cave is a cave inhabited by bats. The caves have high ceilings from which the bats spend a good bit of the day hanging. Of course, all the bat excrement—the "bat guano"—falls to the floor of the cave.

COHEN: That's what bat guano is? Ugh.

WEIROB: Sometimes bats have occupied these caves for a long, long time, hundreds, thousands, maybe even tens of thousands of years. The bat guano builds up until it's incredibly deep, and cockroaches and such thrive in it, so when you go in a bat cave there is this endlessly deep seething mass of bat guano, with the activity of the cockroaches making it seem almost alive.

MILLER: Gretchen, what is the point? Are you trying to win the bet by grossing me out until I have to call it quits?

WEIROB: I'm just explaining this picture. The photographer came across this bat cave because he heard a baby bat's chirp. The baby bat had slipped from the ceiling of the cave, fallen into the guano, and broken its little baby bat wing. It was quite doomed, pitifully chirping as it sank into the guano while cockroaches were starting to feed on it. If you look closely, you can see that's what the picture is. There is the little bat right there.

COHEN: Oh, my God. Gretchen, that is horrible. What *is* your point?

WEIROB: That little baby bat is suffering as much as our hypothetical bird, caught in the soda bridle I dropped. But the bat isn't suffering on account of anyone's sin or evil or laziness or unfortunate choice. That's why I thought of this case, about as far removed from the effects of human choices as you could want. The cave, the guano, the occasional fall of a baby bat, the cockroaches—these are not the inventions of a demented human being. These are not the effects of human carelessness. This is just the way the system works. If God designed and created the system, it's on his shoulders, not on the shoulders of any of his free creatures.

Now I ask you, *what could he have had in mind,* to create such a system as this system of bats, guano, and cockroaches? Was it for our edification? So that every decade or so a nature photographer could stumble in a bat cave and take a gross picture? How many thousands of baby bats sink to a totally unpleasant death for every picture that comes out of it?

Let me put it this way. You've given us an arguably consistent story of how we can have a world with evil caused by free agents. But there are all kinds of suffering that are *not* caused by free agents. Suffering happens because of the way things work—the way God made things work, if there is a God. This is *natural evil,* or maybe *natural suffering,* for we might not want to call something evil that isn't the result of someone's free choice. *But it is suffering nevertheless,* and it can't be laid at the foot of any free creature except God.

COHEN: Some philosophers have claimed that animals don't really feel pain.

WEIROB: Surely you don't believe that.

COHEN: Well, no, not really. But remember, Sam just has to give a consistent picture. I'm not sure it's inconsistent to suppose that animals don't feel pain.

WEIROB: I guess there are more kinds of absurdity than just inconsistency. But whether animals can feel pain is really beside the point. There is enough human suffering to make my point. Some of this suffering—huge amounts of it—is caused by human actions, and so presumably falls under Sam's free will defense. But much of human suffering is not caused by the acts of other humans; it is simply the result of the way nature works. Earthquakes aren't anyone's fault. Nor is cancer. What about floods that carry away innocent children? Epidemics? Famines? Certainly, sometimes floods and epidemics and famines are caused or made worse by things people do. But there were floods before there were human dams to break, famines before there were human food distribution systems to break down. These things are part of the fabric of the world, part of nature. And I don't see how their presence in a world designed by a perfect God can be explained. To be sure, there is much suffering that is caused by human meanness, laziness, carelessness, greed, envy, and the like. And your free will defense is a clever way to account for it. Well, maybe it's more than clever. Maybe it's deep and profound. But it doesn't account for the suffering that is just a product of nature, whether it's a baby bat or a baby human.

COHEN: I don't want you to think I really thought that animals didn't feel pain.

WEIROB: I didn't think that—I know you were just seeing how the argument might go.

Well, Sam, how is the argument going to go? Are you now going to uncover the third part of your theodicy, and explain all the natural suffering in the world, and help us to see what your gentle, loving, all-mighty, and all-perfect God might have had in mind?

MILLER: Gretchen, I've known you for years, but sometimes you leave me speechless. Are you really so moved by the little bat's suffering? Or are you simply moved by the opportunity to shock me and throw this suffering in my face? I'm very aware of suffering, suffering of all kinds, suffering of humans, suffering of animals, suffering of all sorts. It's not just an abstraction for me, or a picture on the back of a magazine, but part of my job. I minister to those who suffer—and to those who have caused suffering. I think you prefer a world in which all this suffering is for naught, with no explanation, no redress, no compensation, no meaning. I . . .

WEIROB: Sam . . .

MILLER: I know what you are going to say. It's not a matter of preference; it's a matter of argument. To win the bet, I need to appeal to your reason, not wonder at your emotions.

I'm sorry I doubted your feeling for the little bat. I'm sure you feel as bad for it as I do. I guess I thought I detected a little joy for the dialectical possibilities your little bat offered, lurking behind the sincere pity for it.

WEIROB: You probably did, Sam, you probably did.

Actually, what I was going to say was that it is getting on toward lunchtime, and maybe we ought to take a break.

MILLER: Goodness, you are right. I have a lunch meeting I need to get to, so we *will* have to break.

WEIROB: Do you want to admit defeat in the face of natural evil?

MILLER: Oh, certainly not. If it's OK with you we can resume later this afternoon. I get back, say, around three.

WEIROB: Why not?

COHEN: Count me in.

4

THE SECOND AFTERNOON

WEIROB: I trust you had a good lunch, Sam?

MILLER: You can never go wrong at Dorsey's, Gretchen. What did you guys eat?

COHEN: We got wild and crazy and had mushroom soup instead of chicken.

WEIROB: I was in a vegetarian mood.

MILLER: I can see why. Your story about the bat ruined your appetite. There's justice in that.

COHEN: I suspect Gretchen's vegetarian phase won't last.

WEIROB: No, probably not much longer than this flu. Then my carnivorous instincts will return as strong as ever. How odd of God to create a world in which so many things eat each other. People eat cattle and chickens and tiny lambs and fish, cockroaches chew on baby bats. . . .

MILLER: OK, Gretchen, I get the point. You want me to get on with my theodicy and try to deal with your baby bat and all the other natural suffering in the world.

WEIROB: Exactly.

MILLER: As I said, the third part of my theodicy is the one you will like the least. So before submitting myself to your sarcasm, let me just remind you of the rules. I'm supposed to provide a *consistent* story that includes evil of all the sorts we have on earth in a world created by a perfect God. It doesn't have to strike you as plausible, much less true. I don't have to claim it is true. I need only claim that my story is consistent. If there is one way, however far-fetched from your point of view, of putting an all-powerful God and the evil and suffering we see into a larger and clearly consistent story, then there are infinitely many other possibilities totally beyond our imagination, but well within the power of God.

WEIROB: OK, OK, get on with it. What is the third part of your theodicy? Devils and angels and things that go bump in the night and sneak up on little baby bats and make them fall?

MILLER: I wouldn't have put it quite that way, Gretchen, but that is, in fact, the general idea. What reason exists to suppose that the only free creatures God created were humans?

COHEN: Certainly dolphins and whales and many other mammals must be candidates.

MILLER: I suppose so, but that's not exactly what I had in mind. In traditional Christianity there are all kinds of other created creatures with freedom, some of whom fell—that is, committed some sort of original sin as Adam did—some of whom are very powerful and capable of all sorts of things.

COHEN: That's beginning to sound like Manichaeism, with its force of good and force of evil.

MILLER: No, that's not right. In Christian doctrine and lore, the devil was created by God and then fell into sin. The force of evil in Manichaeism was not created by the force of good; these forces coexisted from the beginning.

WEIROB: Isn't the devil's main job to lead people into sin,
           like Faustus and the guy who was a fan of the
           Washington Senators in *Damn Yankees?* What
           has that got to do with natural evil?

MILLER: I suppose the devil has powers not only to
           tempt humans into sin, but to cause any kind of
           mischief he wants. Remember, I'm not bound
           by plausibility or even by any kind of official
           Christian doctrine in this debate. I simply have
           to tell a consistent story. My story can include
           a vice-devil for earthquakes, an assistant-devil
           for making the tops of bat caves slippery, sub-
           devils for famines and floods and the like—all
           creatures created free by God, who choose to
           cause suffering of their own free will.

WEIROB: So your idea is that the world contains the devil
           and who knows how many other free creatures,
           who are out there causing problems for us. So
           that crack in California . . .

COHEN: The San Andreas Fault, which causes all the
           earthquakes?

WEIROB: That's the one. That crack isn't there because
           God just threw the earth together, not caring
           much about what happened. Nor is it that he
           cared but didn't know that the geologic
           processes he used to make the surface of the
           earth would leave it with big cracks that cause
           earthquakes. It's not that he cared and knew
           what would happen, but that it was *the best he
           could do.* No, your God is completely benevo-
           lent, knows everything, and can do anything. So
           those aren't the right explanations. The explana-
           tion is that the devil did it! Or some imp or pol-
           tergeist or whatever! That's great, Sam, really
           great. I not only don't believe that, I don't
           believe that you believe it.

MILLER: Wait a minute, Gretchen. I don't claim to believe it. For one thing, I'm not bound by the details of stories about the devil—the human features, red costume, pointed tail, and the like. The point simply is that there may be all kinds of benign and evil agents, all sorts of forces for good and evil who are exercising their free will in ways that affect the lives of humans and of other animals, even of baby bats. I don't think that is so absurd. But in any case, I certainly don't claim that you will or should believe it. Remember the rules. I just claim that it is a consistent, coherent *possibility*. My position is that if there is *one way* that an all-perfect God *could* have created a world with the evils of this one, if there is *one* coherent plan we, with our finite, feeble, limited intellects, can sketch—however incompletely and inadequately—then there are many, many more such plans. Most of these we cannot imagine. Perhaps some day, in some future life, more will be revealed to us. Perhaps, when that great day comes, even you will grant how beautiful God's plan is. Until then, my theodicy, my amalgam of Christian doctrine and legend, serves not as a *hypothesis,* but merely as a *proof of consistency.* That's all I claim for it. All of your sarcasm, all of your doubts, your no doubt sincere shock at my story with its heavens and hells and devils and imps—all of it is to no avail. The story is consistent. I have won the bet, you have lost, wiggle and protest as you may!

COHEN: Well, Gretchen, those are the rules you agreed to. Sam didn't have to prove that an all-perfect God was the simplest hypothesis, or the most obvious, or even the most plausible. He only had to show that it was possible. I must admit that he seems to have done that. Can you find a contradiction in his story?

WEIROB: There are a few issues left dangling. What exactly is freedom? Does the Cohen-Miller account of God's knowledge really make God omniscient? Does the concept of an afterlife make sense?

COHEN: But in all fairness, Gretchen, we agreed that Sam didn't have to solve all the problems of philosophy—and in each case, you agreed things were clear enough to proceed.

WEIROB: I suppose there's no getting around it. I should never have agreed to those rules—they let Sam and his God off the hook so easily. Right at this moment, I can't say that I see a contradiction in your story, Sam. It is fantastic and absurd. I know you only present it as a proof of possibility, therefore you win. Your proof, however, has not exactly instilled religious fervor in me.

MILLER: That would be hoping for too much, Gretchen. Mine was a defensive task. I and millions of others believe in a God you said was impossible, given plain and indisputable facts about suffering and evil in our world. I wanted only to show that it was possible. That mere possibility is not the source of our faith, but a defense of it.

WEIROB: Against me, the evil atheist.

MILLER: You are hardly an evil anything. You are a philosopher, and you can be very irritating. . . . But I repeat myself.

WEIROB: Ha, ha.

COHEN: Loosen up a little, Gretchen.

WEIROB: Well, Dave, are you satisfied with Sam's account of joy and suffering, good and evil?

COHEN: I didn't say that. I simply said that in my opinion, he won the bet.

Now that you ask, it seems to me that the godly are not the only ones who have some explaining to do. If we think that the world as a whole is something that just happened, that there is no God—if we think all of that, then where do right and wrong, good and bad, virtue and evil, and all the rest of these things come from?

MILLER: That's a good point, Dave. What principles can a thinker like that—a thinker like you, Gretchen, as far as I can tell—appeal to? What makes something wrong? Not that God disapproves. What's your answer to Augustine's question, "How does evil enter the world?"

WEIROB: Well, since you ask, I'll tell you. In fact, you have helped me clarify my own position. It seems to me that I am, in fact, a Manichaean!

MILLER: A Manichaean! Gretchen, I think the flu, and the stress of my forceful and unanswerable arguments, has left you . . .

WEIROB: Don't push it, Sam.

MILLER: . . . tired, and deprived you of your sound judgment. If you think my Christian story is a bit weird, you shouldn't be flirting with Manichaeism. Do you know what the Manichaeans' explanation of the phases of moon was?

WEIROB: Of course I don't, but I have a feeling you are going to tell me.

MILLER: They equated good with light, more or less. As the forces of goodness and light battle with the forces of evil and darkness, the forces of good acquire little bits of light from their victories. Captured territory, so to speak. They store these bits of light in the moon for a month at a time. The phases correspond to the moon filling up and then emptying after it is full. The light is transported to the sun, until the moon is again empty—the new moon.

WEIROB: Well, that's certainly weird, although you have to admit it's rather clever. But I'm not going to worry about that. I'm not a fundamentalist Manichaean. I'm just going for the essence of it.

MILLER: Based on your deep study of it—the bits and pieces I've told you over the last two days!

WEIROB: Exactly. I might not be a great scholar of Manichaeism, but the central idea seems to me exactly right. The world—more specifically, the earth, the place where we live—is a battleground of good and evil. Both forces are very powerful. It's not at all obvious how the battle will turn out.

COHEN: By "evil" do you simply mean suffering? And by "good" something like pleasure or joy?

WEIROB: No, no, it's not that simple. I do think pleasure and pain are the basis of good and evil. The way I see it, there was no good or evil, no joy or suffering, no pleasure or pain, until some kind of sentient being, a being with experiences, evolved. These experiences were, at least in a primitive sense, pleasurable or painful.

COHEN: Would experience necessarily bring pain and pleasure with it?

WEIROB: I don't really think much of anything is *necessary*. But it seems to me that from the point of view of nature, if you'll allow me to speak that way, pleasure and pain are the point of experience. The basic setup of animals on earth is to seek situations that are pleasurable and avoid those that are painful. That's the basic *architecture,* as people say nowadays.

MILLER: The "point of view of nature." Is nature then a sort of god, with purposes and intentions and points of view?

WEIROB: No, that's not what I mean, although it does sound like it. Talking of nature's point of view is only a useful metaphor. The basic processes of evolution, of unplanned accidental variations, propagation of useful traits, survival of the fittest, and all of that, don't require any purpose-giver or Grand Mind in the background. When I say that pleasure and pain are the point of experience from nature's point of view, I mean that when we ask what experiences would give systems that had these experiences some sort of evolutionary advantage, it has to be their painfulness or pleasantness. It is the connection between those characteristics of experience and the nature of the situations in which they occur that makes them useful. Pain warns of danger, pleasure leads us to be attracted to situations useful for the propagation of our genes. They are not perfect signs, but they must be, or at one time must have been, useful enough so that the capacity for them was developed as animals evolved.

I'm no great expert on this, by the way. If this doesn't satisfy you, I'm stumped.

MILLER: No, that's OK. Go ahead and use your metaphor. I really want to understand how you look at these things.

COHEN: Pleasure and pain are fairly reliable signs of situations that are good or bad for a creature to be in?

WEIROB: It may not be the creatures, but the creatures' genes that are really at stake, that evolution really cares about—so to speak. Pleasure and pain are ways of getting creatures to seek and avoid situations, depending on whether the situations are good or bad for their survival—or the probability of their passing on genes, for which their survival, at least for a while, is a necessary condition.

The main thing is that with sentience, with experience, comes pain and pleasure, and they have an evolutionary point. They are signals, however fallible, of what situations to seek and what to avoid. But the sentient creatures don't have to know the meaning of the signals. They just need to avoid the pain and seek the pleasure.

This whole process has, as one might say, transcended itself.

COHEN: "Transcended itself"? That sounds profound and a bit foggy—it doesn't sound like you, Gretchen.

WEIROB: What I'm getting at is pretty simple. Start with pain. Pain is often a sign of danger. When I touch a hot stove, pain is a signal to move my hand. When I cut myself, pain is a signal to get treatment. But there are all kinds of situations in which there is pain, but no action that can be taken to lessen the danger. Pain can also be a useless signal of something wrong, as in the case of the bat that can do nothing about its situation, or the pain of a terminal illness, or of an injury that has already been treated.

A good analogy here, I think, is car alarms.

MILLER: Car alarms?

WEIROB: Car alarms are set up for one thing: to go off if someone is messing with the car in order to steal the car or its contents. If the car is jiggled, the alarm goes off. This prevents theft often enough that car alarms have "found a niche" and more and more people are putting them on their cars—they are "propagating."

MILLER: In spite of the fact that they are extremely loud and irritating, often go off when no theft is occurring, and often are ignored by people who hear them, who, if they are like me, would prefer that all cars with car alarms were stolen and taken away from the neighborhood.

WEIROB: Exactly. Car alarms are only semireliable signs of car theft, but they "propagate" nevertheless. The people who install them are satisfied if alarms go off when the car is in danger. They don't mind, or don't mind enough, if they sound at other times, when there is no danger. Or if they continue to sound, after the car has been broken into, the thief has left, and nothing can be done. Or if they go off when practical jokers jiggle a car that they have no interest in robbing or stealing. Therefore we have car alarms going off in cases where there is nothing to be done, when all the noise they make is utterly useless.

MILLER: So what's the point?

WEIROB: Think of the little bat. Pressure on its wing causes pain, and in a lot of situations, the pain will cause the bat to move the wing, preventing injury and helping the little bat to stay alive until it does whatever bats do to produce more baby bats. Perhaps also the bat's crying gets its mother's attention—I really don't know much

about what it's like to be a bat, so I'm making
this up. But in the case of the little bat that fell,
this mechanism had simply gone crazy, like a
car alarm that is uselessly set off, by an explo-
sion that has pretty much destroyed the car anyway. The bat's wing is already broken; it
couldn't move it, even if the bat weren't stuck in
the guano. But the pain goes on and on.

COHEN: Your picture, then, is this: there is this basic
mechanism in which pain signals danger. It gets
propagated because it's accurate enough to be
useful. But pain also occurs in all sorts of situations in which it does no good. There is a surplus of pain, one might say, all sorts of pain,
serving no evolutionary purpose.

WEIROB: Exactly right. And it seems to me that the intentional causing of such pain, pain that does the
one who feels the pain no good, is basically
what evil is all about. I'm sure this picture has
to be qualified in many ways to be an acceptable theory. We think it's OK to cause one person pain in order to save others even more
pain—at least some pretty careful thinkers do.
Maybe it is, maybe it isn't. Prima facie, as
philosophers like to say, causing pain is evil.
Perhaps evil occurs only in our little corner of
the universe. It requires not only sentient
beings, but beings that have the capacity to figure out what situations cause pain for other
beings and to form intentions to bring about
such situations. But there are plenty of sentient
beings on earth, and enough humans to do all
sorts of evil.

COHEN: How about pleasure? Where does it fit in?

WEIROB: Pleasure is more complicated, perhaps. There is
also a surplus of pleasure.

MILLER: You can't mean that there is too much pleasure, Gretchen. That would be very unlike you!

WEIROB: You're right. "Surplus of pleasure" sounds like I think there is too much. But I mean just what Dave meant when he said "surplus of pain"—

COHEN: That there is pleasure that does not signal that one is in a beneficial situation, for one's survival or the propagation of one's genes.

WEIROB: Right. That's what I mean by it. There is a bit of a conflict there, on which some people put a great deal of weight. I'm told that after copulation a female praying mantis bites off the head of her mate. The copulation was good for the propagation of the male's genetic characteristics, but not for the male. But I digress. As Sam rightly observes, I certainly don't think there is a surplus in the sense that there is too much. I'm all for pleasure.

MILLER: I think I get the idea, but an example would help.

WEIROB: Think of how we eat. Most of us love fat in its various forms. Who knows why things made with fat give rise to such pleasant tastes? Perhaps long ago this mechanism developed because fat was scarce and a very good thing for animals like us to seek out and eat. But we continue to seek the pleasure that comes with eating fat when the need for the fat is gone, our little taste buds shooting off blasts of pleasure as we gorge ourselves on cookies and pastries and steaks and rolls plastered with butter. This pleasure does not signal a situation that is good for us or for our genes.

MILLER: In fact, we now typically assume that if something tastes good, it is bad for us!

WEIROB: That's pretty much right. But of course, why should nature care if we die of hardening of the arteries or obesity or some other fat-induced problem, as long as it takes long enough to kill us that we have had a good chance to "propagate our genes."

COHEN: So in your theory, is good the causing of extra pleasure, pleasure that is not a signal of some situation that is beneficial for oneself or propagating one's genes?

WEIROB: No, that wouldn't be quite right, would it? It certainly is good to prevent pointless pain, as well as to promote pointless pleasure. And certainly promoting pleasure that is a signal that one is in a beneficial situation is prima facie OK. Well, let me remind you that I'm not trying to come up with "Gretchen's ethical theory" on the fly here. I'm just trying to provide a simple picture of what, it seems to me, must be at the bottom of the topics I've been giving Sam's religion a hard time about, suffering and evil.

COHEN: How about this: evil is causing unnecessary pain, or preventing harmless pleasure. Good is causing harmless pleasure, or preventing unnecessary pain.

WEIROB: That's good, and it captures what I'm getting at, though I'm sure your statement would need all kinds of elaboration and qualification. But that's basically how I think of suffering and pleasure, good and evil. They are accidents. Pain and pleasure are a strategy that evolution hit upon— metaphorically speaking, Sam—no doubt quite by accident, not as part of any grand design. Good and evil are human concepts that we use to classify intentional action. They are very complicated concepts, and the forms of human pain and pleasure are incredibly diverse and complex. The simple formula Dave gave is much too simple. But I do believe that any reasonable theory of good and evil will ultimately trace these concepts to how acts promote pain and pleasure, suffering and joy. So good and evil are a double accident: first the accident of sentience; second, the accidents that led to the evolution of complex intentional activity of the sort humans engage in.

MILLER: Good and evil are just human inventions, then?

WEIROB: The concepts of good and evil are human inventions. So are the concepts of number, animal, vegetable and mineral, star and planet. That doesn't mean that numbers, animals, vegetables, minerals, stars, and planets were our invention. Things of all those sorts existed long before we came along, and we would not have come along if they hadn't existed. They are real aspects of the world that, as far as we know, only humans have an elaborate enough life to need concepts for. Maybe good and evil are like that.

COHEN: But Gretchen, as I understand your theory, not only are the concepts human inventions, but the aspects we use the concepts to classify are also things that don't exist without humans. The concepts of good and evil classify human activities, right? It sounds to me like you are coming close to saying that good and evil are human inventions, whether you want to or not.

WEIROB: I admit it sounds like that. Maybe it *is* that. I think this is another question we should pursue some day, the whole question of when something is real, and when it is just a human invention. Just remember, locomotives are human inventions. But if one hits you, you will think it is real enough.

But my main point is that whether or not good and evil are just human inventions, it is on earth that good and evil acts occur. And it is certainly a battleground, with lots of good things and lots of evil things happening every day. So in that sense, I am a Manichaean.

MILLER: I'm not sure this rather dismal picture of things is enough to make you a Manichaean.

WEIROB: Well, I guess I'm not, in the sense that I don't think that good and evil are the basic forces in the universe as a whole. But I am in that I think what's important about the universe is the sentient beings in it, which as far as I know or ever will know are all right here on earth. So good and evil are pretty basic forces in the important part of the universe. And like the Manichaeans, I don't think evil is a creation of good, or vice versa.

MILLER: Manichaean or not, it seems to me a dark picture of the world. Are you sure you don't prefer my picture, silly as you think it is? Wouldn't you prefer to live in a world in which our thoughts and actions had some higher meaning, where all the things we value most, sentience, consciousness, thought, intention, and virtue aren't simply the result of blind processes? As I understand your picture, all that we think of as good, all sacrifice, all art, all culture, all knowledge, and philosophy itself, are the result of processes that once conferred some evolutionary advantage but have since run wild.

WEIROB: My view is certainly something like that. But let me remind you, even if good and evil are products of human activity, what is good is good;

what is noble is noble; what isn't, isn't. I don't deny that some things are good or noble and others are evil and base, nor do I say that it is an unimportant distinction.

MILLER: I prefer my mysterious world, with an all-powerful God whose plan we cannot understand, to your picture of human life as a process run amok in a meaningless world.

WEIROB: And you are free to do so! It is your right and privilege. Also, I'm afraid, you have another right and privilege, that of saying a prayer for me, since you seem to have won the bet.

COHEN: I suggest we have dinner at Dorsey's. Sam can say his prayer there, before we eat. Our fellow citizens will be very amused to see Gretchen bow her head.

WEIROB: As a form of humiliation, I suppose that is relatively restrained.

MILLER: Are you feeling well enough to go out, Gretchen?

WEIROB: Yes, I think so. Two days of friends and philosophy are a wonderful tonic. A few aspirin didn't hurt either, and they don't seem to have upset my stomach. Dorsey's will be fun. But if I sneeze in the middle of your prayer, Sam, you mustn't accuse me of impiety.

MILLER: Why, Gretchen, the thought would never occur to me.

NOTES

Augustine's *Confessions* is a fascinating work. He recounts his struggle with the intellectual problem of evil and with giving up what he came to regard as a life of sin after he converted from Manichaeism to Christianity. Augustine is a tremendously important figure in the history of Christianity, the history of philosophy, and the history of literature. His *Confessions* is the first example of autobiography in which the author focuses on his thoughts, motivations, feelings, and inner life. Augustine wrote many other works that consider various aspects of the problem of evil; see especially his *On the Free Choice of the Will.*

David Hume's *Dialogues Concerning Natural Religion* is another historically important and readable work that considers the problem of evil. The considered opinion of Philo, the character who seems to speak for Hume, is that evil is not logically inconsistent with the existence of an all-powerful God, but without some antecedent and unshakable belief in such a God, the evidence of evil would argue overwhelmingly against a benevolent God. Philo concludes that the "cause or causes of order in the universe probably bear some remote analogy to human intelligence," but that it is most likely that that cause (or those causes) does not care one way or another about the suffering of humans and other animals. At one point Philo advances a view that anticipates some of the themes of the theory of evolution (a century before Darwin), and explains the adaptation of animals to their environment by the survival of the fittest rather than by the design and beneficence of God. In the end Philo decides the evolutionary view is absurd.

A number of interesting articles on the problem of evil by twentieth-century philosophers and additional references can be found in the anthologies listed in Further Reading. John Fischer's introduction to *God, Foreknowledge and Freedom* is a valuable guide to much of this literature. Miller's defense of the claim that he doesn't have to argue that this is the best of all possible worlds is taken from Robert Adams's article, "Must God Create the Best," which is reprinted in his *The Virtue of Faith.*

FURTHER READING

Adams, Robert. *The Virtue of Faith.* Oxford: Oxford University Press, 1987.

Augustine. *Confessions.* Indianapolis: Hackett Pub. Co., 1993.

Augustine. *On the Free Choice of the Will.* Indianapolis: Hackett Pub. Co., 1993.

Fischer, John Martin, ed. *God, Foreknowledge and Freedom.* Stanford: Stanford University Press, 1989.

Hume, David. *Dialogues Concerning Natural Religion.* Indianapolis: Hackett Pub. Co., 1998. Second edition.

Pike, Nelson, ed. *God and Evil.* Englewood Cliffs, N.J.: Prentice-Hall, 1964.

Tomberlin, James E., ed. *Philosophical Perspectives*: Vol. 5, *Philosophy of Religion.* Atascadero, Calif.: Ridgeview, 1991.